Introduction

This is the story of the big, speedy fullback Franco Harris, who helped turn a losing team, the Pittsburgh Steelers, into Super Bowl champions.

It is also the story of the people who helped Franco to become the fine person and the star that he is today—his high school and college coaches, his father and his Italian mother, who is so delightful that some of this story is about her.

Franco Harris

S. H. Burchard

Illustrated with photographs

Harcourt Brace Jovanovich
New York and London

For Gina Harris and Bill Gordon

PHOTO CREDITS
United Press International, cover, pp. 6, 43, 51, 53, 56, 58, 62, 64.
Pittsburgh Steelers, p. 2.
Gina Harris, pp. 9, 10, 11, 12, 14, 16, 27.
Sue Burchard, pp. 15, 19, 30, 32, 33, 41.
Bill Gordon, p. 21.
Ken Brewer, *Burlington County Herald*, pp. 23, 25, 28.
Pennsylvania State University, Still Photography Services, pp. 35, 37, 39, 45.
Pittsburgh Chamber of Commerce, p. 46.

Frontispiece: Running back Franco Harris of the Pittsburgh Steelers

Library of Congress Cataloging in Publication Data
Burchard, S   H
   Sports star, Franco Harris.

SUMMARY: An easy-to-read biography of the big, speedy fullback who helped turn the Pittsburgh Steelers into Super Bowl champions.
   1. Harris, Franco, 1950-   —Juvenile literature.
2. Football—Juvenile literature.   [1. Harris, Franco, 1950-
2. Football—Biography]   I. Title.
GV939.H33B87   796.33′2′0924 [B] [92]   75-35527
ISBN 0-15-278000-9
ISBN 0-15-278005-X pbk.

Contents

1

Cad Meets Gina

There were many American
  soldiers in Europe in 1945.
The United States was fighting
  in World War II.
Soldiers who were serving in
  countries far away from their
  homes often were lonely.
One night in Pisa, Italy, a
  young girl went to a dance.
She was tiny and very pretty.

The famous Leaning Tower of Pisa is
in Pisa, Italy, where Cad Harris met Gina.

She was only 17 years old.
Her name was Gina.
Gina was not looking for a
  boyfriend.
She just liked to dance.
She saw a black American
  soldier standing alone.
Gina thought he looked very
  big and handsome in his
  uniform.
The soldier's name was Cad
  Harris.
Cad asked Gina to dance.
He knew only a few words of
  Italian, but Gina smiled at
  everything he said.
Gina and Cad fell in love.

8

Two years later they decided to
    get married.
They were married in an
    Italian church.

Gina Harris in her wedding dress

Cad Harris

Some time later they came to
the United States on a big
ship filled with soldiers.
Cad and Gina Harris lived on
many army posts.

Franco

Their first child, Daniella, was
born in Chicago, Illinois.
Mario was born in Battle
Creek, Michigan.
Franco was born in Fort Dix,
New Jersey.

Then the Harris family moved
to a three-bedroom apartment
in nearby Mount Holly, New
Jersey, where they lived for
twelve years.

Cad Harris retired from the army and got a job taking charge of the dining room in an army hospital.

He worked hard and was good to his wife and children.

The family kept growing until there were nine children.

After Franco came Marisa, Alvara, Luana, Piero, Giuseppe, and finally Michele.

Gina and Cad did not mind taking care of their big family.

Their children were very important to them.

Franco and Mario in front of their apartment in Mount Holly, New Jersey

Franco plays in a pool
with his brother and sisters.

They did not have much
   money, but they were a very
   happy family.
When Mario and Franco were
   in grade school, they started
   to play football.
One day the boys brought their
   uniforms home to be washed.

14

Franco started playing football
   at the Samuel Miller School.

Gina Harris had never heard of
   the game of football.
"What are these ugly things?"
   she asked her sons.
"This is a football suit, Mom,"
   said Franco.
Gina Harris never had time to
   watch her sons play football.
She was too busy cooking and
   cleaning and washing
   clothes.

Gina Harris and some of her children:
(left to right) Franco, Mario,
Alvara, Marisa, and Daniella

2

High School Fullback

Many black soldiers brought
home white brides after
World War II and lived near
army bases such as the one at
Fort Dix.
Franco and his brothers and
sisters did not feel strange
because their father was
black and their mother was
white.

Some of their friends were the children of mixed marriages, too.

The people living in Mount Holly were poor, but most of them wanted the best for their children.

They made sure their town had good schools.

The Harris children all went to the Rancocos Valley High School.

Franco made the varsity football team in his second year.

He was big and strong and could run fast, so he played fullback.

18

The Rancocos Valley High School

Coach Bill Gordon could see
　that Franco was a great
　athlete, but there was one
　problem.
The whole Harris family liked
　to sleep late.

19

Franco missed the first
morning practice because he
was sleeping.
He did not show up until the
afternoon.
When he missed the next
morning's practice, Coach
Gordon got angry.
He went to Franco's house to
lay down the law.
"Football is a team sport," he
told Franco as the whole
family listened.
"If you want to play, you must
be on time."
Franco was never late for
practice again.

Coach Bill Gordon

He became very serious about
the game.
He took good care of his body
so that he stayed strong.
Sometimes he stayed late at
night to practice.
He usually did not have
enough money to take the
bus home.
It took him half an hour to
walk home.
Often he arrived home cold
and dirty.
Gina Harris decided that she
wanted to know more about
the game that meant so much
to her son.

22

Franco Harris (No. 32)
running with the ball

So she went to Franco's first
  game.
Mario was also on the team.
The first time he got the ball,
  Franco ran for 80 yards.

Gina Harris still did not
    understand the game.
She could not see the numbers
    on the uniforms, so she could
    not pick out her sons.
She stood up when others
    stood up.
Cad told her when touchdowns
    were made.
By his third year in high
    school, Franco was the
    biggest player on the team.
He was six feet two inches tall
    and weighed 205 pounds.
He led the Rancocos Red
    Devils to an undefeated
    season.

Franco picks up more yards
    for the Red Devils.

The whole town was pleased
with the team's record.
One father took the players to a
fancy restaurant and treated
the boys to all the steak they
could eat.
In his senior year Franco was
named the team captain.
He was good at thinking up
plays that gained many yards.
He was the leader of the team.
The Red Devils were league
champions for the second
year in a row.
Franco was also on the first
team in baseball and
basketball.

26

The Mount Holly basketball team.
Franco is kneeling at the left.

But he liked football best.
By the middle of his senior
  year, Franco began to get
  scholarship offers from many
  colleges—Cornell, Syracuse,
  Temple, Boston College,

Penn State, Ohio State, Notre
Dame, Michigan, Michigan
State, and the University of
Pittsburgh.
Franco was not only a great
player.
He was also a fine student.

Gina and Cad Harris asked
    Coach Gordon for advice on
    picking the right college for
    Franco.
They were very proud of their
    famous son.
But they were also proud of
    their other eight children.

High school senior Franco Harris
sporting his new mustache

3

College Star

One day Franco walked into
   Bill Gordon's office.
"Well, Coach," he said.
"I have decided on Penn
   State."
Coach Gordon thought it was a
   good choice.
Penn State had great teams and
   a great football coach—Joe
   Paterno.

The Penn State campus

Franco could also get a good
education at Penn State.
In the fall of 1968, the Harris
family and Coach Gordon
drove Franco to the Penn
State campus in the rolling
hills of western
Pennsylvania.

The Harris family drove through many miles
of rolling farmland to get to Penn State.

It was a big day for Gina
 Harris.
She had spent all of her
 married life raising children
 and washing clothes.
It was her first trip away from
 home.
It was her first night in a hotel.

The Nittany Lion Inn, where Gina Harris
spent her first night away from home

Coach Paterno and Gina Harris
  liked each other at once.
They were both Italian.
Franco was of course not
  allowed to play on the varsity
  until his second year at Penn.
In the meantime, he studied
  hard and got good grades.
He had many friends.
Girls liked him because he was
  such a gentleman and was
  very handsome.
Football is a big sport at Penn
  State.
The school is very proud of its
  winning teams and Coach
  Paterno.

The Penn State football stadium at half time

When Franco started his
sophomore year, the Penn
State Nittany Lions were
rated the number two team
in the country.

Coach Paterno had great hopes
  for his two new running
  backs—Franco Harris and
  another New Jersey player,
  Lydell Mitchell.
He was not disappointed.
In the opening game each
  rookie scored a touchdown.
The Lions were a great
  running team.
In the middle of the season,
  Penn State met their old
  rivals, Syracuse University.
At half time the Lions were
  losing by a score of 14 to 0.
It looked like the end of Penn's
  15-game winning streak.

Franco Harris (No. 34)
pushes for a bigger gain.

Then, in the third quarter,
   Lydell Mitchell ran for a
   touchdown.
Franco smashed over the goal
   line for two more points.

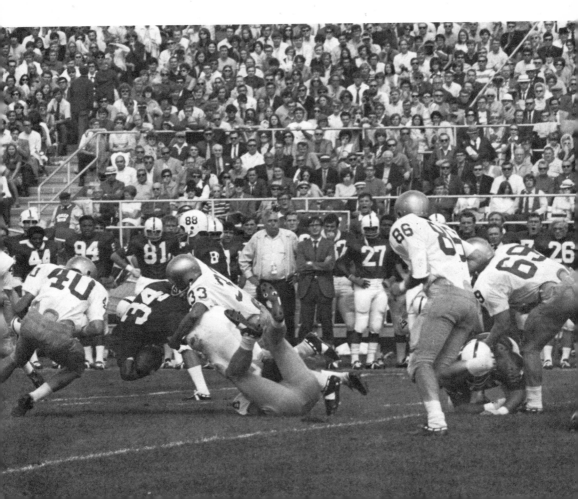

With only a few minutes to go,
Franco broke loose and ran
for a 36-yard touchdown.
The play made him a hero.
The score was 14 to 14.
The crowd went wild.
The extra point was good.
Penn State won by a score of
15 to 14.
It was perhaps Penn State's
greatest victory because they
came from so far behind.
The Nittany Lions had one of
their best years ever and
their second undefeated
season in a row.
Franco scored in every game.

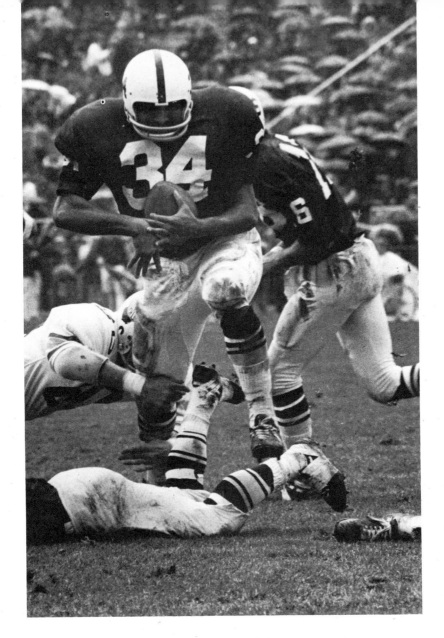

Franco runs over one player and drags
another behind him in a Penn game.

In the opening game of
Franco's junior year, the
Lions clobbered Navy by a
score of 55 to 7.

Then came the upset.

The Penn State team went to
Colorado to play the Colorado
Buffaloes in front of national
television and lost by a score
of 41 to 13.

When the sleepy players
climbed off the buses at
3:00 A.M. the morning after
the disaster, they were
amazed to see a crowd of
2,000 people standing in the
darkness to welcome them.

Penn State was still number
  one in their hearts.
"I've been at Penn State for 20
  years," said Coach Paterno.
"And I have never been
  prouder of a team than I am
  at this moment."

Coach Joe Paterno

The crowd cheered.
"And I have never been
    prouder of a student body!"
    he added.
Penn State lost two more
    games that season.
Franco had an injured ankle
    and could not play his best.
The next year—Franco's senior
    year—the Penn State team
    wanted to start their winning
    streak all over again.
Franco taught the new players
    things he had learned.
Coach Paterno liked the way
    Franco got along with his
    teammates.

Led by the two All-American running backs, Harris and Mitchell, Penn State scored the first four times they had the ball in the first game of the season and beat Navy by a score of 56 to 3.

Franco Harris (No. 34) leaps over teammate Lydell Mitchell (No. 23) to pick up a first down against Navy.

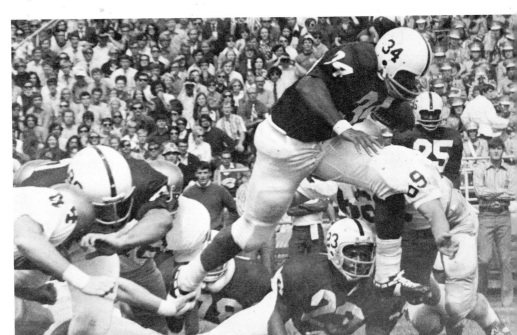

The Lions kept on winning.
But in the middle of the season
Franco began to be bothered
by sore ribs.
When they would hurt too
much, he would leave the
game.
He felt stronger by the end of
the season.
Penn State won every game
except the last one.
They lost to Tennessee by a
score of 31 to 11.
The Harris family came to
many of the games.
Gina Harris still did not know
what was going on.

But she could feel the
 excitement.
Her All-American son was
 wanted by many pro teams.

Franco Harris of Penn State

The city of Pittsburgh

4

A Lucky Bounce

Pittsburgh is a city known for
its steel mills and gray
buildings.
A cigar-chewing little man
named Art Rooney bought
the Steelers for the
sports-loving people of
Pittsburgh in 1933.
He paid only $2,500 for the
team.

For 39 years Mr. Rooney and
Pittsburgh football fans
suffered.
The Steelers lost more than
they won nearly every
season.
They were never champions of
their division.
Fans stopped going to the
games.
But Mr. Rooney never gave up
on his team.
Before the 1972 season Art
Rooney was more excited
than usual.
The Steelers had a tough new
coach—Chuck Noll.

48

The team had a strong defense
led by "Mean" Joe Greene.
The quarterback, Terry
Bradshaw, was calling better
plays.
And the big college running
back Franco Harris had just
joined the team.
"We were looking for someone
with size, speed, and
catching ability," said Coach
Noll.
"Franco was our man."
He certainly was—but not right
away.
Franco did not play until
Pittsburgh's sixth game.

He didn't get going until the
  seventh.
Then—wham!
He really got moving.
He crashed out 134 yards in a
  big win against the Kansas
  City Chiefs.
He rolled for 128 yards in a
  victory over the tough
  Minnesota Vikings.
That included a 12-yard
  touchdown gallop and a
  61-yard sprint that set up
  another score.
"It's unbelievable how he gets
  away from tacklers," said the
  Viking coach.

50

Franco Harris carries the ball on a muddy field.

"Just when you think you have
   him stopped, he rips away
   for 20 yards."
Pittsburgh fans went crazy.
At long last they had a winning
   team.

Franco became the idol of
  "Steel City."
Since his mother is Italian and
  his father was in the army,
  his fans call themselves
  Franco's Italian Army.
Franco loves his "troops."
"It shows that people really
  care about the team and the
  players," he says.
An Italian who runs a big
  bakery in Pittsburgh had
  ladies make red, white, and
  green Italian flags for the
  rooting section.
One of Franco's fans was
  Coach Noll.

Members of "Franco's Italian Army" do
a little dance after Harris makes a 61-yard run.

"He wants to do well," he said.
"He wants to be the best there
is."
For the first time in 39 years,
the Steelers got into the
play-offs for the American
Conference title.

The Steelers played the
Oakland Raiders in the first
of two play-off games.
With a little over a minute left
in the game, Oakland was
ahead by a score of 7 to 6.
The fans were glum.
The Steelers had the ball on
their 20-yard line.
Quarterback Bradshaw threw
five straight passes.
With ten seconds to go,
Bradshaw threw a blind pass
down the field in the general
direction of Steeler Frenchy
Fuqua.

Fuqua leaped for the ball, but
he was knocked hard from
behind by Raider Jack
Tatum.
The ball came down, hit
Tatum, and took a seven-yard
backward bounce.
Franco had seen the ball fly
over his head, and then
suddenly it came back near
his knees.
With five seconds to go, Franco
scooped up the ball and took
off at full speed.
He ran 42 yards for the
winning touchdown.

The Steelers reached their dressing room in a daze. Most of them did not know what had happened.

In one of the strangest plays in the history
of football, a last-minute Bradshaw
pass bounces off Raider Jack Tatum
and into the arms of rookie Franco Harris,
who runs 42 yards for the winning touchdown.

"I didn't see the ball bounce
    away," Bradshaw said.
"I just saw Franco roar off.
I've played football since
    second grade.
Nothing like that ever
    happened.
It'll never happen again.
And to think it happened here
    in Pittsburgh in a play-off!"
But Pittsburgh's joy did not
    last.
The following Sunday they lost
    the American Conference
    title to the Miami Dolphins.

5

Super Bowl Champions

For the second year in a row,
  the Steelers made the
  play-offs.
Again they clashed against the
  Oakland Raiders.
But this time they lost.
At the start of the 1974 football
  season the Steelers were
  stronger than ever.
They won game after game.

59

Franco Harris dives over the
goal line for a touchdown.

Once more they made the
   play-offs.
The Steelers faced the Buffalo
   Bills in the first round.
The Pittsburgh defense
   stopped cold star running
   back O. J. Simpson.
The offense made 26 points in
   the second quarter.
Franco scored three
   touchdowns in 15 minutes.
The Steelers won by a score of
   32 to 14.
Then, for the third year in a
   row, Pittsburgh met the
   Oakland Raiders in the
   play-off series.

They won and became
American Conference
Champions, but then they
had the biggest game of all
ahead of them.
They had to meet the National
Conference champions, the
Minnesota Vikings, in the
Super Bowl for the National
Football League
championship.
Led by "Mean" Joe Greene,
the Steeler defense kept the
Vikings from running and
passing.
But no one could stop Franco.
He was too strong.

He pushed his way through the
purple-shirted Vikings all
afternoon.

In spite of its being a bitter
cold day with winds up to 25
miles per hour, Franco did
an amazing amount of
standing up and running.
A crowd of 80,997 sat shivering
in the stands and saw Franco
break two bowl records.
He was the first back to gain
over 150 yards in a Super
Bowl contest.
He was also the first to carry
the ball as many as 34 times.
The Steelers won by a score of
16 to 6.
They were National Football
League champions.

In the third quarter of the
Super Bowl, Franco fumbles but recovers
for a nine-yard gain.

A very happy Pittsburgh coach, Chuck Noll,
is carried off the field by Franco and
Joe Greene after the Super Bowl victory.

Red, white, and green flags
waved all over the stadium.
A tiny Italian lady, who by now
knew a great deal about
football, sat next to her big
husband and smiled.